McGraw-Hill/Contemporary

A Division of The McGraw·Hill Companies



Send all inquiries to:
McGraw-Hill/Contemporary
4255 W. Touhy Ave.
Lincolnwood, IL 60712



ISBN: 0-07-252757-9

Printed in the United States of America.

2 3 4 5 6 7 8 9 10 HCM 08 07 06 05 04 03 02

# TABLE OF CONTENTS

# TABLE OF CONTENTS

# TABLE OF CONTENTS (CONT.)

The CASIO *fx*-260 SOLAR calculator

1 Your calculator is only a tool to help perform calculations. You must decide what numbers and operations to use to solve a problem.

2 Become familiar with the calculator keys and operations to build your skill and speed.

3 Always estimate the answer to a problem before you begin to do the calculations. Check your answer against your estimate.

# Using Your CASIO *fx*-260 SOLAR Calculator

1

# Correcting a Keying Error

2

Four ways to correct an error:

1 To correct a mistake when you have not pressed a [+] [−] [×] or [÷] key, use the backspace key [▶].

**EXAMPLE** 1572 + 56 =

**STEP 1** Enter [1] [5] [6] [2]. To correct, press [▶] [▶], and reenter [7] [2].

2 To clear the last number entry, press the [C] key.

**EXAMPLE** 2647 − 328 =

**STEP 1** Enter [2] [6] [4] [7] [−] [5] [6]. To correct, press [C], and reenter [3] [2] [8].

3 To change an incorrect operation key ( + − × or ÷ ), simply press the correct operation key to override.

**EXAMPLE** $448 + 369 =$

**STEP 1** Enter 4 4 8 −. To correct, press +, and continue with the calculation.

---

4 To clear everything and start the calculation all over again, press the AC key.

**EXAMPLE** $588 \times 72 =$

**STEP 1** Enter 5 8 7 × 7 2. To correct, press AC, and start all over again.

# Adding Whole Numbers



**EXAMPLE** 658 + 469 =

| | |
|---|---|
| **STEP 1** | Enter 6 5 8. |
| **STEP 2** | Press the + key. |
| **STEP 3** | Enter 4 6 9. |
| **STEP 4** | Press the = key. The display will show 1127.. |
| **ANSWER** | **1,127** |

Press AC to clear the display.

## Practice

1 Attendance figures for three basketball games were as follows: Thursday 3,904, Friday 2,179, and Saturday 1,946. How many tickets were sold for these three games?

2 The weight of the children in the Thomas family are Steven, 72 pounds; Gail, 98 pounds; Jeff, 114 pounds; Sally, 124 pounds; and Jenny, 135 pounds. What is the sum of the weights of the Thomas children?

### ANSWERS

1 8,029 tickets

2 543 pounds

# Subtracting Whole Numbers



**EXAMPLE** 1,241 – 529 =

**STEP 1** Enter 1 2 4 1.

**STEP 2** Press the – key.

**STEP 3** Enter 5 2 9.

**STEP 4** Press the = key. The display will show 712..

**ANSWER** **712**

Press AC to clear the display.

# Practice

1 The Nile River is 4,160 miles long. The Congo River is 2,900 miles long. How much longer is the Nile River than the Congo River?

2 In 1900 the population in Asia was 932,000. In 1998 the population had grown to 3,528,000. How much was the increase in population from 1900 to 1998?

**ANSWERS**

1 1,260 miles

2 2,596,000 people

# Multiplying Whole Numbers



**EXAMPLE** $3{,}025 \times 24 =$

**STEP 1** Enter 3 0 2 5.

**STEP 2** Press the × key.

**STEP 3** Enter 2 4.

**STEP 4** Press the = key. The display will show 72600..

**ANSWER** **72,600**

Press AC to clear the display.

## Practice

1 Sound travels at 1,129 feet per second. How far away was a thunderbolt that took 8 seconds to reach the ear of the listener?

2 A pilot flies his airplane at an average speed of 415 miles per hour. How far can he fly in 12 hours?

### ANSWERS

1 9,032 feet

2 4,980 miles

# Dividing Whole Numbers



**EXAMPLE** $4{,}284 \div 6 =$

**STEP 1** Enter 4 2 8 4.

**STEP 2** Press the ÷ key.

**STEP 3** Enter 6.

**STEP 4** Press the = key. The display will show 714..

**ANSWER** **714**

Press AC to clear the display.

# Practice

1 If Frank types at the rate of 55 words per minute, how many minutes will it take him to type a report containing 1,760 words?

2 Audrey works at a book store. There are 32,040 books packed in cartons. If each carton has 36 books, how many cartons will Audrey unpack?

**ANSWERS**

1 32 minutes

2 890 cartons

# Adding Decimals



**EXAMPLE** 547.69 + 243.63 =

**STEP 1** Enter [5] [4] [7] [.] [6] [9].

**STEP 2** Press the [+] key.

**STEP 3** Enter [2] [4] [3] [.] [6] [3].

**STEP 4** Press the [=] key. The display will show [791.32].

**ANSWER** **791.32**

Press [AC] to clear the display.

# Practice

1 At a picnic, two tables were placed end to end. If the first table is 2.89 meters long and the second is 1.94 meters long, what is the combined length of the two tables?

2 Monday Michael drove 268.3 miles. Tuesday he drove 353.8 miles. Wednesday he drove 226 miles, and Thursday he drove 242.7 miles. What total distance did Michael drive those 4 days?

**ANSWERS**

1 4.83 meters

2 1,090.8 miles

# Subtracting Decimals



**EXAMPLE** $50.3 - 5.89 =$

**STEP 1** Enter 5 0 . 3.

**STEP 2** Press the − key.

**STEP 3** Enter 5 . 8 9.

**STEP 4** Press the = key. The display will show 44.41.

**ANSWER** **44.41**

Press AC to clear the display.

# Practice

1 Ming is trying to decide which of two pork roasts to buy. One weighs 4.79 pounds, and the other weighs 6.2 pounds. How much heavier is the larger roast than the smaller one?

2 Normal September rainfall is 1.24 inches in Denver and 7.63 inches in Miami. How much more rainfall does Miami get in September?

**ANSWERS**

1 1.41 pounds
2 6.39 inches

# Multiplying Decimals



**EXAMPLE** $15.4 \times 2.19 =$

**STEP 1** Enter 1 5 . 4.

**STEP 2** Press the × key.

**STEP 3** Enter 2 . 1 9.

**STEP 4** Press the = key. The display will show 33.726.

**ANSWER** **33.726**

Press AC to clear the display.

# Practice

1 The distance between Mustafa's house and his office is 2.85 miles. He walks this distance twice each day, Monday through Friday. How many total miles does Mustafa walk each week between his house and work?

2 In the metric system, weight is measured in units called grams. If 28.4 grams is equal to 1 ounce, how many grams does an 11-ounce steak weigh?

**ANSWERS**

1 28.5 miles

2 312.4 grams

# Dividing Decimals



**EXAMPLE** $104.748 \div 11.6 =$

| | |
|---|---|
| **STEP 1** | Enter 1 0 4 . 7 4 8. |
| **STEP 2** | Press the ÷ key. |
| **STEP 3** | Enter 1 1 . 6. |
| **STEP 4** | Press the = key. The display will show 9.03. |
| **ANSWER** | **9.03** |

Press AC to clear the display.

# Practice

1 A train traveled 144.4 miles in 4.8 hours. To the nearest mile per hour, what was the average speed of the train?

2 One inch is equal to 2.54 centimeters. How many inches are there in 27.94 centimeters?

**ANSWERS**

1 30 mph

2 11 inches

# Expressing a Remainder as a Whole Number



**EXAMPLE** A process uses 7 gallons of fluid for each batch. The fluid comes in 65 gallon drums. After the batches are made from one drum, how many gallons of fluid are left over?

**STEP 1** Enter the division problem. Press the [=] key to get the quotient. [6] [5] [÷] [7] [=] [9.285714286].

**STEP 2** Subtract the whole number part of the answer. [−] [9] [=] [0.285714285].

**STEP 3** Multiply the decimal part of the answer by the original divisor. [×] [7]

**STEP 4** Press the [=] key. The display will show [2.].

**ANSWER** **2 gallons of fluid are left over after 9 batches are made.**

Press [AC] to clear the display.

# Practice

1 A machinist has a piece of wood that measures 140 inches. He needs to cut 6-inch pieces from the wood. After the pieces are cut, what is the length of the remaining piece of wood?

2 Nathan agreed to remove 224 cubic yards of gravel from a building site. Assuming he carries 11 cubic yards for each full load, how many cubic yards of gravel will Nathan carry on his final load?

**ANSWERS**

1 2 inches

1 4 cubic yards

# Rounding to a Specified Number of Digits



**EXAMPLE** Divide 23 by 18. Round your answer to the nearest thousandth.

**STEP 1** Enter 2 3 ÷ 1 8 =.

**STEP 2** The display will show 1.277777778.

**STEP 3** Press the MODE key and the 7 key.

**STEP 4** Press the number of decimal places you want to round to 3.

**STEP 5** The word FIX will appear in the display. The display will show 1.278.

**ANSWER** **1.278**

Press ON to clear the mode function and display.

## Practice

1 Divide 1,293 by 172. Round your answer to the nearest hundredth.

2 Divide 598 by 27. Round your answer to the nearest thousandth.

3 Divide 4 by 6. Round your answer to the nearest ten-thousandth.

**ANSWERS**

1 7.52

2 22.148

3 0.6667

# Rounding Money to the Nearest Cent



**EXAMPLE** If sales tax is 7.25%, how much tax is paid on $198.98?

**STEP 1** Enter [ . ] [ 0 ] [ 7 ] [ 2 ] [ 5 ].

**STEP 2** Press the [ × ] key.

**STEP 3** Enter [ 1 ] [ 9 ] [ 8 ] [ . ] [ 9 ] [ 8 ].

**STEP 4** Press the [ = ] key. The display will show [ 14.42605 ].

**STEP 5** Press [ MODE ] [ 7 ] [ 2 ].
The display will show [ 14.43 ].

**ANSWER** **$14.43**

Press [ ON ] to clear the mode function and display.

## Practice

1 The price of gasoline is $1.439. To the nearest cent, what will Kerri pay for 12.8 gallons of gas?

2 Vicki paid $31.71 for a roast. If the roast weighed 5.78 pounds, how much did Vicki pay per pound? Round your answer to the nearest cent.

**ANSWERS**

1 $18.42

2 $5.49

# Reducing Fractions



**EXAMPLE** Reduce $\frac{125}{1000}$ to lowest terms.

**STEP 1** Enter the numerator [1] [2] [5].

**STEP 2** Press the [a b/c] key.

**STEP 3** Enter the denominator [1] [0] [0] [0].

**STEP 4** Press the [=] key. The display will show [1⌋8.].

**ANSWER** $\frac{1}{8}$

Press [AC] to clear the display.

# Practice

Reduce these fractions to lowest terms.

1 $\frac{16}{20}$

2 $\frac{15}{8}$

3 $\frac{16}{40}$

**ANSWERS**

1 $\frac{4}{5}$

2 $1\frac{7}{8}$

3 $\frac{2}{5}$

# Adding Fractions



**EXAMPLE** $2\frac{2}{3} + \frac{3}{5} =$

**STEP 1** Enter 2 a b/c 2 a b/c 3 .

**STEP 2** Press the + key.

**STEP 3** Enter 3 a b/c 5 .

**STEP 4** Press the = key. The display will show 3⌋4⌋15. .

**ANSWER** $3\frac{4}{15}$

Press AC to clear the display.

# Practice

1 Matt bought $2\frac{1}{2}$ pounds of apples and $6\frac{2}{3}$ pounds of cherries. How much fruit did he buy?

2 Maxine spent $1\frac{1}{2}$ hours driving on Thursday, $2\frac{2}{3}$ hours driving on Friday, and $3\frac{5}{6}$ hours driving on Saturday. How many hours did Maxine drive those 3 days?

**ANSWERS**

1 $9\frac{1}{6}$ pounds

2 8 hours

# Subtracting Fractions



**EXAMPLE** $1\frac{1}{2} - \frac{5}{6} =$

**STEP 1** Enter 1 a b/c 1 a b/c 2.

**STEP 2** Press the − key.

**STEP 3** Enter 5 a b/c 6.

**STEP 4** Press the = key. The display will show 2⌋3..

**ANSWER** $\frac{2}{3}$

Press AC to clear the display.

# Practice

1 Margaret had a piece of material 10 yards long. She used $2\frac{3}{4}$ yards to make a pillow and $4\frac{2}{5}$ yards to make a cover for her sofa. How much material was left?

2 Verzell changed the speed of his cement mixer from $6\frac{1}{3}$ rpm's to 10 rpm's. By how many revolutions per minute did the mixer speed increase?

**ANSWERS**

1 $2\frac{17}{20}$ yards

2 $3\frac{2}{3}$ rpm

# Multiplying Fractions



**EXAMPLE** $2\frac{3}{4} \times \frac{7}{8} =$

**STEP 1** Enter [2] [a b/c] [3] [a b/c] [4].

**STEP 2** Press the [×] key.

**STEP 3** Enter [7] [a b/c] [8].

**STEP 4** Press the [=] key. The display will show [2⌋13⌋32.].

**ANSWER** $2\frac{13}{32}$

Press [AC] to clear the display.

# Practice

1 As an apprentice electrician, Lalo makes \$15 an hour. How much would Lalo make for $3\frac{1}{4}$ hours of work?

2 One cubic foot of water weighs $62\frac{1}{2}$ pounds. How much do $4\frac{3}{5}$ cubic feet of water weigh?

**ANSWERS**

1 $\$48\frac{3}{4}$ or \$48.75

2 $287\frac{1}{2}$ pounds

# Dividing Fractions



**EXAMPLE** $\frac{2}{5} \div 2\frac{1}{4} =$

**STEP 1** Enter 2 a b/c 5.

**STEP 2** Press the ÷ key.

**STEP 3** Enter 2 a b/c 1 a b/c 4.

**STEP 4** Press the = key. The display will show 8⌟45..

**ANSWER** $\frac{8}{45}$

Press AC to clear the display.

# Practice

1 On a test Adriano got $\frac{7}{8}$ of the problems correct. He had 21 problems correct. How many problems were on the test?

2 A tailor needs $3\frac{3}{4}$ yards of material to make a suit for his daughter. How many suits can he make from $12\frac{1}{2}$ yards of material?

## ANSWERS

1 24 problems

2 $3\frac{1}{3}$, or 3 complete suits

# Changing Fractions to Decimals



**EXAMPLE** Change $\frac{40}{250}$ to a decimal.

**STEP 1** Enter the numerator 4 0.

**STEP 2** Press the ÷ key.

**STEP 3** Enter the denominator 2 5 0.

**STEP 4** Press the = key. The display will show 0.16.

**ANSWER** **0.16**

Press AC to clear the display.

# Practice

Change these fractions to decimals.

1 $\frac{3}{9}$

2 $\frac{7}{8}$

3 $\frac{15}{8}$

**ANSWERS**

1 0.333 . . .

2 0.875

3 1.875

# Finding the Part Using the % Key



**EXAMPLE** Find 35% of 500.

| | |
|---|---|
| **STEP 1** | Enter the whole [5] [0] [0]. |
| **STEP 2** | Press the [×] key. |
| **STEP 3** | Enter the percent number [3] [5]. |
| **STEP 4** | Press the [SHIFT] key and the [%] key (above the [=] key). |
| **STEP 5** | The display will show [175.]. |
| **ANSWER** | **175** |

Press [AC] to clear the display.

# Practice

1 If your hourly pay rate is $7.50 and you get a 3% raise, what is the amount of your increase per hour?

2 You see a pair of $58 slacks with a tag that says 25% off. By how much is the price of the slacks reduced?

### ANSWERS

1 22.5 cents per hour

2 $14.50

# Finding the Whole Using the % Key



**EXAMPLE** 42 is 70% of what number?

**STEP 1** Enter the part 4 2.

**STEP 2** Press the ÷ key.

**STEP 3** Enter the percent number 7 0.

**STEP 4** Press the SHIFT key and the % key (above the = key).

**STEP 5** The display will show 60.

**ANSWER** **60**

Press AC to clear the display.

## Practice

1 Tuition at a community college went up 15% for an increase of $12 per credit hour. Before the increase, what was the tuition per credit hour?

2 In just over three months, Amy lost 40 pounds. If Amy lost 20% of her weight, how much did she originally weigh?

**ANSWERS**

1 $80

2 200 pounds

# Finding the Percent Using the % Key



**EXAMPLE** 12 is what percent of 60?

**STEP 1** Enter the part [1] [2].

**STEP 2** Press the [÷] key.

**STEP 3** Enter the whole [6] [0].

**STEP 4** Press the [SHIFT] key and the [%] key (above the [=] key).

**STEP 5** The display will show [20.].

**ANSWER** **20%**

Press [AC] to clear the display.

## Practice

1 Mr. Park makes a down payment of $2,100 on a new car that costs $15,995. To the nearest percent, what percent did he make as a down payment?

2 After paying his bills this month, Bernie has $426 left from a monthly paycheck of $2,154. To the nearest percent, what percent of Bernie's paycheck did not go for paying bills?

**ANSWERS**

1 13%

2 20%

# Adding a Percent of a Number



**EXAMPLE** A sweater sells for $19.98. If the sales tax is 6%, what is the purchase price of the sweater?

**STEP 1** Enter the whole number [1] [9] [.] [9] [8].

**STEP 2** Press the [×] key.

**STEP 3** Enter the percent number [6].

**STEP 4** Press the [SHIFT] key and the [%] key (above the [=] key).

**STEP 5** Press the [+] key. The display will show [21.1788].

**ANSWER** **$21.18**

Press [AC] to clear the display.

## Practice

1 Shelley has a part-time job. In June she is getting a 7% raise. What will Shelley's monthly salary be in June if now she is making $860 per month?

2 Puffy Pet Products places a 15% markup on every item they sell. How much will Puffy Pet Products charge for a bag of dog food that cost them $18.40?

**ANSWERS**

1 $920.20

2 $21.16

# Subtracting a Percent of a Number



**EXAMPLE** A television sells for $298. At a 20%-off sale on electronics, what is the sale price of the TV?

**STEP 1** Enter the whole number [2] [9] [8].

**STEP 2** Press the [×] key.

**STEP 3** Enter the percent number [2] [0].

**STEP 4** Press the [SHIFT] key and the [%] key (above the [=] key).

**STEP 5** Press the [−] key. The display will show [238.4].

**ANSWER** **$238.40**

Press [AC] to clear the display.

## Practice

1 After new speed limits went into effect this year, traffic accidents decreased by 20% each month. How many traffic accidents occurred this July if 75 accidents occurred last July?

2 At a Memorial Day sale, Glenda saw a coat marked with two tags. One read, "Price $84.00." The other read, "Take an additional 20% off the marked price." If she buys the coat, what can Glenda expect to pay?

**ANSWERS**

1 60 accidents

2 $67.20

# Finding Percent of Increase



**EXAMPLE** Last month Lee's salary was raised from $8.80 per hour to $10.20 per hour. What percent raise did Lee receive? Round your answer to the nearest percent.

**STEP 1** Subtract to find the amount of increase.
[1] [0] [.] [2] [−] [8] [.] [8] [=] [1.4].

**STEP 2** Divide by the original amount. [÷] [8] [.] [8]

**STEP 3** Press the [SHIFT] key and the [%] key (above the [=] key).

**STEP 4** The display will show [15.90909091].

**ANSWER** **16%**

Press [AC] to clear the display.

# Practice

1 Between 1995 and 2001, the value of Erica's condominium increased from $55,600 to $68,200. What percent of value increase is this? Round your answer to the nearest percent.

2 Between December 1 and March 1, the average weekly snowfall in Newton increased from 0.5 inches to 1.2 inches. What percent of increase in snowfall does this change represent?

**ANSWERS**

1 23%

2 140%

# Finding Percent of Decrease



**EXAMPLE** Cora's Cottons reduced the price of a sweater from $42.50 to $32.95. What percent of price reduction is this? Round your answer to the nearest percent.

**STEP 1** Subtract to find the amount of decrease.
[4] [2] [.] [5] [−] [3] [2] [.] [9] [5] [=] 9.55.

**STEP 2** Divide by the original amount. [÷] [4] [2] [.] [5]

**STEP 3** Press the [SHIFT] key and the [%] key (above the [=] key).

**STEP 4** The display will show 22.47058824.

**ANSWER** **22%**

Press [AC] to clear the display.

# Practice

1 In the past 5 years, the population of Farm Grove decreased from 84,600 to 72,100. What percent of population decrease does this change represent? Round your answer to the nearest percent.

2 For the weekend, Barry's Bakery lowers the price of coffee cake from $3.29 to $2.85. What percent of price decrease is this price reduction? Round your answer to the nearest percent.

**ANSWERS**

1 15%

2 13%

# Using Memory



**EXAMPLE** Find the total cost of 2 pens at $0.15 each and 3 notebooks at $1.15 each.

**STEP 1** Enter 2 × . 1 5.

**STEP 2** Press the M+ key.

**STEP 3** Enter 3 × 1 . 1 5.

**STEP 4** Press the M+ key.

**STEP 5** Press the MR key for the total.
The display will show 3.75.

**ANSWER** **$3.75**

Press ON to clear the memory function and display.

# Practice

1 Marci's regular job pays $10.50 an hour for 40 hours a week. She also has a part-time job that pays $7.50 an hour for 15 hours a week. What is Marci's total weekly salary?

2 Matt is buying 50 feet of lumber at $3.15 per running foot and 13 feet of baseboard at $2.19 per running foot. What is his total bill, not counting sales tax?

**ANSWERS**

1 $532.50

2 $185.97

# Finding Squares



**EXAMPLE** Find the area of a square with sides 4 feet long. ($A = s^2$)

**STEP 1** Enter the number to be squared [4].

**STEP 2** Press the [$x^2$] key.

**STEP 3** The display will show [16.].

**ANSWER** **16 square feet**

Press [AC] to clear the display.

# Practice

1 Find the area of a square garden that is 21 yards on each side.

2 Jennifer is covering a square table with glass. How much glass will be needed if the table measures 45 centimeters on each side?

**ANSWERS**

1 441 square yards

2 2,025 square centimeters

# Finding Cubes



**EXAMPLE** Find the volume of a cube with sides 6 feet long. ($V = s^3$)

**STEP 1** Enter the number to be cubed [6].

**STEP 2** Press the [SHIFT] key.

**STEP 3** Press the [$x^3$] key (above the [▶] key).

**STEP 4** The display will show [216.].

**ANSWER** **216 cubic feet**

Press [AC] to clear the display.

# Practice

1 Compute the volume of a storage room that has a square floor 7 meters on each side and is 7 meters high.

2 How many cubic yards of sand will it take to fill an excavation that measures 14 yards long, 14 yards wide, and 14 yards deep?

**ANSWERS**

1 343 cubic meters

2 2,744 cubic yards

# Finding Higher Powers



**EXAMPLE** Find $4^5$.

**STEP 1** Enter the base 4.

**STEP 2** Press the $x^y$ key.

**STEP 3** Enter the exponent 5.

**STEP 4** Press the = key. The display will show 1024..

**ANSWER** **1,024**

Press AC to clear the display.

## Practice

Find the value of each power.

1 $9^4$

2 $(5.5)^5$

3 $8^6$

**ANSWERS**

1 6,561

2 5,032.84375

3 262,144

# Finding Square Roots



**EXAMPLE** Find $\sqrt{90}$ to the nearest tenth.

**STEP 1** Enter the number for which you want to find the square root [9] [0].

**STEP 2** Press the [SHIFT] key.

**STEP 3** Press the [$\sqrt{\ }$] key (above the [$x^2$] key).

**STEP 4** The display will show [9.486832981].

**ANSWER** **9.5**

Press [AC] to clear the display.

## Practice

Find the value of each square root to the nearest tenth.

1 $\sqrt{120}$

2 $\sqrt{456}$

3 $\sqrt{118}$

**ANSWERS**

1 11.0

2 21.4

3 10.9

# Finding Cube Roots



**EXAMPLE** Find $\sqrt[3]{100}$ to the nearest tenth.

**STEP 1** Enter the number for which you want to find the cube root [1] [0] [0].

**STEP 2** Press the [SHIFT] key.

**STEP 3** Press the [$\sqrt[3]{\ }$] key (above the [+/−] key).

**STEP 4** The display will show [4.641588834].

**ANSWER** **4.6**

Press [AC] to clear the display.

# Practice

Find the value of each cube root to the nearest tenth.

1 $\sqrt[3]{645}$

2 $\sqrt[3]{189}$

3 $\sqrt[3]{96}$

**ANSWERS**

1 8.6

2 5.7

3 4.6

# Adding Signed Numbers



**EXAMPLE** $-9 + 5 =$

**STEP 1** Enter 9.

**STEP 2** Press the +/− key.

**STEP 3** Press the + key.

**STEP 4** Enter 5.

**STEP 5** Press the = key. The display will show −4..

**ANSWER** **−4**

Press AC to clear the display.

# Practice

Add these signed numbers.

1 $-5 + 8 + (-14) =$

2 $-4.5 + (-18.36) + 2.12 =$

3 $5\frac{1}{8} + (-6\frac{3}{4}) =$

**ANSWERS**

1 $-11$

2 $-20.74$

3 $-1\frac{5}{8}$

# Subtracting Signed Numbers



**EXAMPLE** $-6 - (-8) =$

| | |
|---|---|
| **STEP 1** | Enter 6. |
| **STEP 2** | Press the +/− key. |
| **STEP 3** | Press the − key. |
| **STEP 4** | Enter 8. |
| **STEP 5** | Press the +/− key. |
| **STEP 6** | Press the = key. The display will show 2.. |
| **ANSWER** | **2** |

Press AC to clear the display.

# Practice

Subtract these signed numbers.

1 $-3 - 45 =$

2 $-4.5 - (-10.99) =$

3 $25\frac{1}{4} - (-32\frac{7}{8}) =$

**ANSWERS**

1 $-48$

2 $6.49$

3 $58\frac{1}{8}$

# Multiplying Signed Numbers



**EXAMPLE** $-4 \times (-7) =$

| | |
|---|---|
| **STEP 1** | Enter **4**. |
| **STEP 2** | Press the **+/−** key. |
| **STEP 3** | Press the **×** key. |
| **STEP 4** | Enter **7**. |
| **STEP 5** | Press the **+/−** key. |
| **STEP 6** | Press the **=** key. The display will show 28.. |
| **ANSWER** | **28** |

Press **AC** to clear the display.

# Practice

Multiply these signed numbers.

1 $-14 \times (-24) =$

2 $5.75 \times (-0.1) =$

3 $-3\frac{5}{6} \times \frac{3}{5} =$

**ANSWERS**

1 336

2 −0.575

3 $-2\frac{3}{10}$

# Dividing Signed Numbers



**EXAMPLE** $-8 \div (-4) =$

**STEP 1** Enter 8.

**STEP 2** Press the +/− key.

**STEP 3** Press the ÷ key.

**STEP 4** Enter 4.

**STEP 5** Press the +/− key.

**STEP 6** Press the = key. The display will show 2. .

**ANSWER** 2

Press AC to clear the display.

# Practice

Divide these signed numbers.

1 $-33 \div 22 =$

2 $-43.2 \div (-12) =$

3 $-24\frac{1}{2} \div (-20) =$

**ANSWERS**

1 $-1.5$

2 $3.6$

3 $1\frac{9}{40}$

# Solving Equations with $\pi$



**EXAMPLE** Find the area of a circle with radius $\frac{5}{8}$ inches. Round your answer to the nearest hundredth. ($A = \pi r^2$)

**STEP 1** Press the SHIFT key. Then press the $\pi$ key (above the EXP key).

**STEP 2** Press the × key.

**STEP 3** Enter the number for the radius 5 a b/c 8.

**STEP 4** Press the $x^2$ key.

**STEP 5** Press the = key. The display will show 1.22718463.

**ANSWER** **1.23 square inches**

Press AC to clear the display.

# Practice

1 Find the circumference of a circular fish pond with a diameter of 20 feet. ($C = \pi d$)

2 Find the volume of a cylinder that is 10 inches high and has a radius of 3 inches. ($V = \pi r^2 h$)

3 Find the volume of a cone that is 9 inches high and has a radius of 4 inches. ($V = \frac{1}{3}\pi r^2 h$)

**ANSWERS**

1 62.8 feet

2 282.6 cubic inches

3 150.72 cubic inches

# Solving Equations with ( )



**EXAMPLE** Solve for $x$: $x = 4(\frac{3}{4} - 1) + (-5)$

**STEP 1** Enter [4] and press the [×] key.

**STEP 2** Press the [(--- key. The display will show [ [0 1  0. ].

**STEP 3** Enter the expression [3] [a b/c] [4] [−] [1].

**STEP 4** Press the ---)] key. The display will show [ −1⌟4. ].

**STEP 5** Press the [+] key and enter [5]. Press the [+/−] key.

**STEP 6** Press the [=] key. The display will show [ −6. ].

**ANSWER** $x = -6$

Press [AC] to clear the display.

# Practice

Solve these equations for $x$.

**1** $x = 2(-4 + 3 - 7)$

**2** $x = 6 + 5(-3 \times 5)$

**ANSWERS**

**1** $x = -16$

**2** $x = -69$

# Solving Equations with ( ) and [ ]



**EXAMPLE** $-3[6 + 8(2 - 5)] =$

| | |
|---|---|
| **STEP 1** | Enter 3. Press the +/− key and × key. |
| **STEP 2** | Press the [(--- key. The display will show [01 0.. |
| **STEP 3** | Enter the expression 6 + 8 and press the × key. |
| **STEP 4** | Press the [(--- key. The display will show [02 0.. |
| **STEP 5** | Enter the expression 2 − 5. |
| **STEP 6** | Press the ---)] key twice and press the = key.<br>The display will show 54.. |
| **ANSWER** | **54** |

Press AC to clear the display.

## Practice

Solve these equations.

1 $\frac{3(9 + 5) - 10}{5} =$

**Hint:** Begin and end the entire numerator with [ ].

2 $4[15 - 3(24 - 55)] =$

### ANSWERS

1 6.4

2 432

# Trigonometric Functions



**EXAMPLE** A transit reading was taken at ground level 25 feet from a tree. The angle was 50°. To the nearest foot, how tall is the tree?

**STEP 1** Write an equation for (tangent = $\frac{\text{opposite side}}{\text{adjacent side}}$) $\tan 50° = \frac{x}{25}$.

**STEP 2** Enter [5] [0] and press the [tan] key.
The display will show [1.191753593].

**STEP 3** Press the [×] key and enter [2] [5].

**STEP 4** Press the [=] key. The display will show [29.79383981].

**ANSWER** **30 feet**

Press [AC] to clear the display.